100 DAYS OF

WALKING BY FAITH

devotional journal

N. Niami

100 DAYS OF WALKING BY FAITH

Copyright © 2021 by Noor Niami

All rights reserved. This book or any portion thereof may not be reproduced or used in any manner whatsoever without the express written permission of the publisher except for the use of brief quotations in a book review.

Published by: Noor Niami

For information contact:
Noor Niami
www.noorniami.com

First Printing, 2021
ISBN: 978-0-6489327-7-2 (paperback)

All Scripture quotations, unless otherwise indicated, are taken from the Holy Bible, New International Version®, NIV®. Copyright ©1973, 1978, 1984, 2011 by Biblica, Inc.™ Used by permission of Zondervan. All rights reserved worldwide. www.zondervan.comThe "NIV" and "New International Version" are trademarks registered in the United States Patent and Trademark Office by Biblica, Inc.™

To

_____

From

_____

Date

_____

Introduction

Our walk with God is a walk of faith for we walk by faith and not by sight. We are also told that without faith it is impossible to please God so having faith is crucial in every believer's life. As much as you want to plan your life, remember that God is the One who orders your steps. God has a way of surprising you with unexpected things that make you happier than you originally intended. Sometimes the bad things that happen in our lives put us directly on the path to the best things that will ever happen to us. Have faith that everything will work itself out because it will. You don't need to know the details of what, when, how, or where, you just need to relax and believe that things will fall into place and make perfect sense at the perfect time. Your job isn't to have it all figured out but to believe everything is unfolding according to God's perfect plan for your life. Your faith will require you to see beyond what is happening, your faith will require you to call those things that are not as though they are. Speak victory over your battle. Speak peace over your chaos. Speak healing over your pain. Things can be crumbling down and you still have the ability to believe that something great is on the urge of happening. Have faith in God, have faith in yourself, and have faith in life. All is well, relinquish control, surrender, let go, accept what is, and have faith in what will be.

As you begin your journey of 100 days of biblical truth about God's love for you have faith and believe that God's plans will exceed your plans in the most beautiful and amazing ways. Let go and let God amaze you because He abounds in goodness, grace, and mercy.

With love & light,

Noor Niami

And it is impossible to
please God without faith.
Anyone who wants to come
to him must believe that
God exists and that he
rewards those who
sincerely seek him.

Hebrews 11:6

And do not be conformed to this world, but be transformed by the renewing of your mind, that you may prove what is that good and acceptable and perfect will of God.

Romans 12:2

LOVE

Love

I am a child of God

> See what great love the Father has lavished on us, that we should be called children of God! And that is what we are! The reason the world does not know us is that it did not know him.
>
> **1 JOHN 3:1**

Daily Devotion

Day 1

Date: ___,_____,_____

How can I apply this to my life?
_____
_____
_____
_____
_____
_____

What is God saying through this Scripture?
_____
_____
_____
_____
_____
_____

I praise the Lord for...
_____
_____
_____
_____
_____
_____

PRAYER REQUESTS   **ANSWERED PRAYERS**

Today's Affirmation

I am a child of the Most High God, I belong to Him.

Love

I am loved.

I have been crucified with Christ and I no longer live, but Christ lives in me. The life I now live in the body, I live by faith in the Son of God, who loved me and gave himself for me.

GALATIANS 2:20

Daily Devotion

Day 2

Date: ____._____._____

How can I apply this to my life?
_____
_____
_____
_____
_____
_____

What is God saying through this Scripture?
_____
_____
_____
_____
_____
_____

I praise the Lord for...
_____
_____
_____
_____
_____
_____

PRAYER REQUESTS   **ANSWERED PRAYERS**

Today's Affirmation

I am worthy of love because of what Christ has done for me.

Love

I am rejoiced over.

> The Lord your God is with you, the Mighty Warrior who saves. He will take great delight in you; in his love he will no longer rebuke you, but will rejoice over you with singing."

ZEPHANIAH 3:17

Daily Devotion

Day 3

Date: ___._____,_____

How can I apply this to my life?
_____
_____
_____
_____
_____
_____

What is God saying through this Scripture?
_____
_____
_____
_____
_____
_____

I praise the Lord for...
_____
_____
_____
_____
_____
_____

PRAYER REQUESTS   ANSWERED PRAYERS

Today's Affirmation

My God delights in me and I in Him, I am rejoiced over.

Love

God thinks good thoughts of me.

For I know the plans I have for you," declares the Lord, "plans to prosper you and not to harm you, plans to give you hope and a future.

JEREMIAH 29:11

Daily Devotion

Day 4

Date: ___._____._____

How can I apply this to my life?
_____
_____
_____
_____
_____
_____

What is God saying through this Scripture?
_____
_____
_____
_____
_____
_____

I praise the Lord for...
_____
_____
_____
_____
_____
_____

PRAYER REQUESTS   **ANSWERED PRAYERS**

Today's Affirmation

I am safe in God's hands, His plans will prosper me.

Love

I am never alone.

When you pass through the waters, I will be with you; and when you pass through the rivers, they will not sweep over you. When you walk through the fire, you will not be burned; the flames will not set you ablaze.

ISAIAH 43:2

Daily Devotion

Day 5

Date: ___._____._____

How can I apply this to my life?
_____
_____
_____
_____
_____
_____

What is God saying through this Scripture?
_____
_____
_____
_____
_____
_____

I praise the Lord for...
_____
_____
_____
_____
_____
_____

PRAYER REQUESTS   **ANSWERED PRAYERS**

Today's Affirmation

I am never alone because God is with me everywhere I go.

Love

He knows my name.

But now, this is what the Lord says— he who created you, Jacob, he who formed you, Israel: "Do not fear, for I have redeemed you; I have summoned you by name; you are mine.

ISAIAH 43:1

Daily Devotion

Day 6

Date: ____._____._____

How can I apply this to my life?
_____
_____
_____
_____
_____
_____

What is God saying through this Scripture?
_____
_____
_____
_____
_____
_____

I praise the Lord for...
_____
_____
_____
_____
_____
_____

PRAYER REQUESTS   **ANSWERED PRAYERS**

Today's Affirmation

God knows me by my name, His love for me is personal.

Love

His love never fails.

Though the mountains be shaken and the hills be removed, yet my unfailing love for you will not be shaken nor my covenant of peace be removed," says the LORD, who has compassion on you.

ISAIAH 54:10

Daily Devotion

Day 7

Date: ___._____._____

How can I apply this to my life?
_____
_____
_____
_____
_____
_____

What is God saying through this Scripture?
_____
_____
_____
_____
_____
_____

I praise the Lord for...
_____
_____
_____
_____
_____
_____

PRAYER REQUESTS   **ANSWERED PRAYERS**

Today's Affirmation

Nothing can separate me from the love of God, His love endures forever.

Love

Nothing can separate one from His love.

No, in all these things we are more than conquerors through him who loved us. For I am convinced that neither death nor life, neither angels nor demons, neither the present nor the future, nor any powers, neither height nor depth, nor anything else in all creation, will be able to separate us from the love of God that is in Christ Jesus our Lord.

ROMANS 8:37-39

Daily Devotion

Day 8

Date: ___,_____,_____

How can I apply this to my life?
_____
_____
_____
_____
_____

What is God saying through this Scripture?
_____
_____
_____
_____
_____

I praise the Lord for...
_____
_____
_____
_____
_____

PRAYER REQUESTS

ANSWERED PRAYERS

Today's Affirmation

I am more than a conqueror through Jesus Christ.

Love

I have been saved by His grace.

> But because of his great love for us, God, who is rich in mercy, made us alive with Christ even when we were dead in transgressions— it is by grace you have been saved.
>
> EPHESIANS 2:4-5

Daily Devotion

Day 9

Date: ___._____._____

How can I apply this to my life?
_____
_____
_____
_____
_____
_____

What is God saying through this Scripture?
_____
_____
_____
_____
_____
_____

I praise the Lord for...
_____
_____
_____
_____
_____
_____

PRAYER REQUESTS   **ANSWERED PRAYERS**

Today's Affirmation

I am a new creation in Jesus Christ.

Love

Love is the answer to everything in life.

Love is patient, love is kind. It does not envy, it does not boast, it is not proud. It does not dishonor others, it is not self-seeking, it is not easily angered, it keeps no record of wrongs. Love does not delight in evil but rejoices with the truth. It always protects, always trusts, always hopes, always perseveres.

1 CORINTHIANS 13:4-7

Daily Devotion

Day 10

Date: ____,_____,_____

How can I apply this to my life?
_____
_____
_____
_____
_____
_____

What is God saying through this Scripture?
_____
_____
_____
_____
_____
_____

I praise the Lord for...
_____
_____
_____
_____
_____
_____

PRAYER REQUESTS   **ANSWERED PRAYERS**

Today's Affirmation

I choose love above all else because God is love and love is from God.

I am blessed

HOPE

Hope

My hope in God will not put one to shame.

Not only so, but we also glory in our sufferings, because we know that suffering produces perseverance; perseverance, character; and character, hope. And hope does not put us to shame, because God's love has been poured out into our hearts through the Holy Spirit, who has been given to us.

ROMANS 5:3-5

Daily Devotion

Day 11

Date: ___._____,_____

How can I apply this to my life?
_____
_____
_____
_____
_____
_____

What is God saying through this Scripture?
_____
_____
_____
_____
_____
_____

I praise the Lord for...
_____
_____
_____
_____
_____
_____

PRAYER REQUESTS   **ANSWERED PRAYERS**

Today's Affirmation

Our sufferings produces perseverance, character and hope.

Hope

In all things, God is with one and for one.

And we know that in all things God works for the good of those who love him, who have been called according to his purpose.

ROMANS 8:28

Daily Devotion

Day 12

Date: ____,_____,_____

How can I apply this to my life?
_____
_____
_____
_____
_____

What is God saying through this Scripture?
_____
_____
_____
_____
_____

I praise the Lord for...
_____
_____
_____
_____
_____

PRAYER REQUESTS   **ANSWERED PRAYERS**

Today's Affirmation

God is working everything out for my good.

Hope

I wait and hope for what is not yet here.

For in this hope we were saved. But hope that is seen is no hope at all. Who hopes for what they already have? But if we hope for what we do not yet have, we wait for it patiently.

ROMANS 8:24-25

Daily Devotion

Day 13

Date: ___._____._____

How can I apply this to my life?
_____
_____
_____
_____
_____
_____

What is God saying through this Scripture?
_____
_____
_____
_____
_____
_____

I praise the Lord for...
_____
_____
_____
_____
_____
_____

PRAYER REQUESTS   **ANSWERED PRAYERS**

Today's Affirmation

I wait patiently for what is to come because the best is yet to be.

Hope

My God is a big God and He is more than able.

Now to him who is able to do immeasurably more than all we ask or imagine, according to his power that is at work within us,

EPHESIANS 3:20

Daily Devotion

Day 14

Date: ___,_____,_____

How can I apply this to my life?
_____
_____
_____
_____
_____
_____

What is God saying through this Scripture?
_____
_____
_____
_____
_____
_____

I praise the Lord for...
_____
_____
_____
_____
_____
_____

PRAYER REQUESTS	ANSWERED PRAYERS

Today's Affirmation

He is able to do immeasurably more than I can imagine.

Hope

My hope is greater than my sufferings.

And the God of all grace, who called you to his eternal glory in Christ, after you have suffered a little while, will himself restore you and make you strong, firm and steadfast.

1 PETER 5:10

Daily Devotion

Day 15

Date: ____,_____,_____

How can I apply this to my life?
_____
_____
_____
_____
_____
_____

What is God saying through this Scripture?
_____
_____
_____
_____
_____
_____

I praise the Lord for...
_____
_____
_____
_____
_____
_____

PRAYER REQUESTS   **ANSWERED PRAYERS**

Today's Affirmation

I stand firm on God's promise of restoration.

Hope

My God is a God of hope.

> May the God of hope fill you with all joy and peace as you trust in him, so that you may overflow with hope by the power of the Holy Spirit.
>
> ROMANS 15:13

Daily Devotion

Day 16

Date: ___._____._____

How can I apply this to my life?
_____
_____
_____
_____
_____
_____

What is God saying through this Scripture?
_____
_____
_____
_____
_____
_____

I praise the Lord for...
_____
_____
_____
_____
_____
_____

PRAYER REQUESTS

ANSWERED PRAYERS

Today's Affirmation

I overflow with hope by the power of the Holy Spirit.

Hope

The hope I have in Him will renew my strength.

But those who hope in the Lord will renew their strength. They will soar on wings like eagles; they will run and not grow weary, they will walk and not be faint.

ISAIAH 40:31

Daily Devotion

Day 17

Date: ___,_____,_____

How can I apply this to my life?
_____
_____
_____
_____
_____
_____

What is God saying through this Scripture?
_____
_____
_____
_____
_____
_____

I praise the Lord for...
_____
_____
_____
_____
_____
_____

PRAYER REQUESTS   **ANSWERED PRAYERS**

Today's Affirmation

My hope in God renews my strength.

Hope

The Lord delights in me.

**The Lord delights in those who fear him,
who put their hope in his unfailing love.**

PSALM 147:11

Daily Devotion

Day 18

Date: ___,_____,_____

How can I apply this to my life?
_____
_____
_____
_____
_____
_____

What is God saying through this Scripture?
_____
_____
_____
_____
_____
_____

I praise the Lord for...
_____
_____
_____
_____
_____
_____

PRAYER REQUESTS   **ANSWERED PRAYERS**

Today's Affirmation

Above all else I choose to put my hope in God's love for me.

Hope

God has prepared beautiful things for one.

However, as it is written:
"What no eye has seen, what no ear has heard, and what no human mind has conceived"— the things God has prepared for those who love him.

1 CORINTHIANS 2:9

Daily Devotion

Day 19

Date: ___,_____,_____

How can I apply this to my life?
_____
_____
_____
_____
_____
_____

What is God saying through this Scripture?
_____
_____
_____
_____
_____
_____

I praise the Lord for...
_____
_____
_____
_____
_____
_____

PRAYER REQUESTS   **ANSWERED PRAYERS**

Today's Affirmation

God will always exceed my expectations in the most beautiful ways.

Hope

God is doing a new thing in my life.

"Forget the former things; do not dwell on the past. See, I am doing a new thing! Now it springs up; do you not perceive it? I am making a way in the wilderness and streams in the wasteland.

ISAIAH 43:18-20

Daily Devotion

Day 20

Date: ___,_____,_____

How can I apply this to my life?
_____
_____
_____
_____
_____
_____

What is God saying through this Scripture?
_____
_____
_____
_____
_____
_____

I praise the Lord for...
_____
_____
_____
_____
_____
_____
_____

PRAYER REQUESTS   **ANSWERED PRAYERS**

Today's Affirmation

What is coming is going to be bigger and better than what has gone.

I am
worthy

FAITH

Faith

My faith is the key to my answered prayer.

Therefore I tell you, whatever you ask for in prayer, believe that you have received it, and it will be yours.

MARK 11:24

Daily Devotion

Day 21

Date: ___._____._____

How can I apply this to my life?
_____
_____
_____
_____
_____
_____

What is God saying through this Scripture?
_____
_____
_____
_____
_____
_____

I praise the Lord for...
_____
_____
_____
_____
_____
_____
_____

PRAYER REQUESTS

ANSWERED PRAYERS

Today's Affirmation

My faith in God will grant me my answered prayer.

Faith

God is a rewarder of those who believe in Him.

And without faith it is impossible to please God, because anyone who comes to him must believe that he exists and that he rewards those who earnestly seek him.

HEBREWS 11:6

Daily Devotion

Day 22

Date: ___._____,_____

How can I apply this to my life?
_____
_____
_____
_____
_____
_____

What is God saying through this Scripture?
_____
_____
_____
_____
_____
_____

I praise the Lord for...
_____
_____
_____
_____
_____
_____

PRAYER REQUESTS   **ANSWERED PRAYERS**

Today's Affirmation

I choose faith over fear, I choose believing over doubting.

53

Faith

Blessed are those who believe.

Then Jesus told him, "Because you have seen me, you have believed; blessed are those who have not seen and yet have believed."

JOHN 20:29

Daily Devotion

Day 23

Date: ___,_____,_____

How can I apply this to my life?
_____
_____
_____
_____
_____
_____

What is God saying through this Scripture?
_____
_____
_____
_____
_____
_____

I praise the Lord for...
_____
_____
_____
_____
_____
_____

PRAYER REQUESTS   **ANSWERED PRAYERS**

Today's Affirmation

I am blessed because I have chosen to believe without seeing.

Faith

All things are possible through faith.

"If you can'?" said Jesus. "Everything is possible for one who believes."

MARK 9:23

Daily Devotion

Day 24

Date: ___,_____,_____

How can I apply this to my life?
_____
_____
_____
_____
_____
_____

What is God saying through this Scripture?
_____
_____
_____
_____
_____
_____

I praise the Lord for...
_____
_____
_____
_____
_____
_____

PRAYER REQUESTS	ANSWERED PRAYERS

Today's Affirmation

Amazing things will happen for me because I have chosen to believe in Christ.

Faith

By grace through faith.

For it is by grace you have been saved, through faith — and this is not from yourselves, it is the gift of God— not by works, so that no one can boast.

EPHESIANS 2:8-9

Daily Devotion

Day 25

Date: ___,_____,_____

How can I apply this to my life?
_____
_____
_____
_____
_____

What is God saying through this Scripture?
_____
_____
_____
_____
_____

I praise the Lord for...
_____
_____
_____
_____
_____

PRAYER REQUESTS	ANSWERED PRAYERS

Today's Affirmation

I have been saved by His grace through my faith in Him.

Faith

My faith is the evidence, the proof of the things I hope for.

Now faith is confidence in what we hope for and assurance about what we do not see.

HEBREWS 11:1

Daily Devotion

Day 26

Date: ___,_____,_____

How can I apply this to my life?
_____
_____
_____
_____
_____
_____

What is God saying through this Scripture?
_____
_____
_____
_____
_____
_____

I praise the Lord for...
_____
_____
_____
_____
_____
_____

PRAYER REQUESTS   **ANSWERED PRAYERS**

Today's Affirmation

I don't need to see something to know it's real because my faith tells me it is.

Faith

I have faith that can move mountains.

He replied, "Because you have so little faith. Truly I tell you, if you have faith as small as a mustard seed, you can say to this mountain, 'Move from here to there,' and it will move. Nothing will be impossible for you."

MATTHEW 17:20

Daily Devotion

Day 27

Date: ___._____._____

How can I apply this to my life?
_____
_____
_____
_____
_____
_____

What is God saying through this Scripture?
_____
_____
_____
_____
_____
_____

I praise the Lord for...
_____
_____
_____
_____
_____
_____

PRAYER REQUESTS

ANSWERED PRAYERS

Today's Affirmation

My faith in God will make all things possible.

Faith

My faith will get me through everything.

For everyone born of God overcomes the world. This is the victory that has overcome the world, even our faith.

1 JOHN 5:4

Daily Devotion

Day 28

Date: ____,_____,_____

How can I apply this to my life?
_____
_____
_____
_____
_____
_____

What is God saying through this Scripture?
_____
_____
_____
_____
_____
_____

I praise the Lord for...
_____
_____
_____
_____
_____
_____

PRAYER REQUESTS   **ANSWERED PRAYERS**

Today's Affirmation

God will always grant me victory over every battle I face.

Faith

I come boldly to His throne of grace and ask in faith.

But when you ask, you must believe and not doubt, because the one who doubts is like a wave of the sea, blown and tossed by the wind.

JAMES 1:6

Daily Devotion

Day 29

Date: ____._____.____

How can I apply this to my life?
_____
_____
_____
_____
_____
_____

What is God saying through this Scripture?
_____
_____
_____
_____
_____
_____

I praise the Lord for...
_____
_____
_____
_____
_____
_____

PRAYER REQUESTS　　　**ANSWERED PRAYERS**

Today's Affirmation

I will thank God in advance for my answered prayer.

Faith

His goodness and love follow me.

Surely your goodness and love will follow me all the days of my life, and I will dwell in the house of the Lord forever.

PSALM 23:6

Daily Devotion

Day 30

Date: ____._____._____

How can I apply this to my life?
_____
_____
_____
_____
_____
_____

What is God saying through this Scripture?
_____
_____
_____
_____
_____
_____

I praise the Lord for...
_____
_____
_____
_____
_____
_____

PRAYER REQUESTS

ANSWERED PRAYERS

Today's Affirmation

I will always be loved because His goodness and love will be with me everywhere I go.

I am fearless

TRUST

Trust

God will make my paths straight.

Trust in the Lord with all your heart and lean not on your own understanding; in all your ways submit to him, and he will make your paths straight.

PROVERBS 3:5-6

Daily Devotion

Day 31

Date: ____,_____,____

How can I apply this to my life?
_____
_____
_____
_____
_____

What is God saying through this Scripture?
_____
_____
_____
_____
_____

I praise the Lord for...
_____
_____
_____
_____
_____

PRAYER REQUESTS   **ANSWERED PRAYERS**

Today's Affirmation

I choose not to lean on my own understanding but trust God's wisdom instead.

Trust

He will fulfill the desires of my heart.

> Take delight in the Lord,
> and he will give you the desires of
> your heart. Commit your way
> to the Lord; trust in him
> and he will do this.
>
> PSALM 37:4-5

Daily Devotion

Day 32

Date: ___,_____,_____

How can I apply this to my life?
_____
_____
_____
_____
_____
_____

What is God saying through this Scripture?
_____
_____
_____
_____
_____
_____

I praise the Lord for...
_____
_____
_____
_____
_____
_____

PRAYER REQUESTS   **ANSWERED PRAYERS**

Today's Affirmation

I surrender all my desires to God and choose to wait on Him.

Trust

God is my everlasting rock.

You will keep in perfect peace those whose minds are steadfast, because they trust in you. Trust in the Lord forever, for the Lord, the Lord himself, is the Rock eternal.

ISAIAH 26:3-4

/ Daily Devotion

Day 33

Date: ____,_____,_____

How can I apply this to my life?
_____
_____
_____
_____
_____
_____

What is God saying through this Scripture?
_____
_____
_____
_____
_____
_____

I praise the Lord for...
_____
_____
_____
_____
_____
_____

PRAYER REQUESTS   ANSWERED PRAYERS

Today's Affirmation

God will give me perfect peace as I continue to trust in Him.

Trust

Those who trust in the Lord will be blessed.

"But blessed is the one who trusts in the Lord, whose confidence is in him. They will be like a tree planted by the water that sends out its roots by the stream. It does not fear when heat comes; its leaves are always green. It has no worries in a year of drought and never fails to bear fruit."

JEREMIAH 17:7-8

Daily Devotion

Day 34

Date: ____,_____,_____

How can I apply this to my life?
_____
_____
_____
_____
_____
_____

What is God saying through this Scripture?
_____
_____
_____
_____
_____
_____

I praise the Lord for...
_____
_____
_____
_____
_____
_____

PRAYER REQUESTS   ANSWERED PRAYERS

Today's Affirmation

My trust in the Lord will make me bear fruit in all areas of my life.

Trust

He will never leave me nor forsake me.

Those who know your name trust in you, for you, Lord, have never forsaken those who seek you.

PSALM 9:10

Daily Devotion

Day 35

Date: ___._____._____

How can I apply this to my life?
_____
_____
_____
_____
_____
_____

What is God saying through this Scripture?
_____
_____
_____
_____
_____
_____

I praise the Lord for...
_____
_____
_____
_____
_____
_____

PRAYER REQUESTS **ANSWERED PRAYERS**

Today's Affirmation

The Lord is with me and for me, He is faithful.

Trust

I am protected by the Most High God.

The Lord is my strength and my shield; my heart trusts in him, and he helps me. My heart leaps for joy, and with my song I praise him.

PSALM 28:7

Daily Devotion

Day 36

Date: ___,_____,_____

How can I apply this to my life?
_____
_____
_____
_____
_____

What is God saying through this Scripture?
_____
_____
_____
_____
_____

I praise the Lord for...
_____
_____
_____
_____
_____

PRAYER REQUESTS	ANSWERED PRAYERS

Today's Affirmation

I am under God's provision and protection, my heart trusts in Him.

Trust

I am safe with the Lord my God.

Fear of man will prove to be a snare, but whoever trusts in the Lord is kept safe.

PROVERBS 29:25

Daily Devotion

Day 37

Date: ___._____,_____

How can I apply this to my life?
_____
_____
_____
_____
_____
_____

What is God saying through this Scripture?
_____
_____
_____
_____
_____
_____

I praise the Lord for...
_____
_____
_____
_____
_____
_____
_____

PRAYER REQUESTS   **ANSWERED PRAYERS**

Today's Affirmation

My trust in God will cast out fear, my faith in Him will give me rest.

Trust

God and I are a majority.

When I am afraid, I put my trust in you. In God, whose word I praise— in God I trust and am not afraid. What can mere mortals do to me?

PSALM 56:3-4

Daily Devotion

Day 38

Date: ___._____._____

How can I apply this to my life?
_____
_____
_____
_____
_____
_____

What is God saying through this Scripture?
_____
_____
_____
_____
_____
_____

I praise the Lord for...
_____
_____
_____
_____
_____
_____

PRAYER REQUESTS   **ANSWERED PRAYERS**

Today's Affirmation

When God is for me who can then be against me?

Trust

He hears me and will do it for me.

> This is the confidence we have in approaching God: that if we ask anything according to his will, he hears us. And if we know that he hears us—whatever we ask—we know that we have what we asked of him.
>
> **1 JOHN 5:14-15**

Daily Devotion

Day 39

Date: ___._____._____

How can I apply this to my life?
_____
_____
_____
_____
_____
_____

What is God saying through this Scripture?
_____
_____
_____
_____
_____
_____

I praise the Lord for...
_____
_____
_____
_____
_____
_____

PRAYER REQUESTS

ANSWERED PRAYERS

Today's Affirmation

I am confident that the Lord has heard my prayer and will do it according to His will.

Trust

The Lord is my refuge and my fortress.

Whoever dwells in the shelter of the Most High will rest in the shadow of the Almighty. I will say of the Lord, "He is my refuge and my fortress, my God, in whom I trust."

PSALM 91:1-2

Daily Devotion

Day 40

Date: ___._____._____

How can I apply this to my life?
_____
_____
_____
_____
_____
_____

What is God saying through this Scripture?
_____
_____
_____
_____
_____
_____

I praise the Lord for...
_____
_____
_____
_____
_____
_____

PRAYER REQUESTS   **ANSWERED PRAYERS**

Today's Affirmation

I dwell in the shelter of the Most High, in Him I find rest for my soul.

I am grateful

PATIENCE

Patience

Giving up is not an option.

Let us not become weary
in doing good, for at the proper time we
will reap a harvest if we do not give up.

GALATIANS 6:9

Daily Devotion

Day 41

Date: ___,_____,_____

How can I apply this to my life?
_____
_____
_____
_____
_____
_____

What is God saying through this Scripture?
_____
_____
_____
_____
_____
_____

I praise the Lord for...
_____
_____
_____
_____
_____
_____

PRAYER REQUESTS **ANSWERED PRAYERS**

Today's Affirmation

God is about to do something amazing in my life.

Patience

The Lord will do it at the perfect time.

*Be still before the Lord
and wait patiently for him;
do not fret when people succeed
in their ways, when they carry out
their wicked schemes.*

PSALM 37:7

Daily Devotion

Day 42

Date: ____,_____,_____

How can I apply this to my life?
_____
_____
_____
_____
_____
_____

What is God saying through this Scripture?
_____
_____
_____
_____
_____
_____
_____

I praise the Lord for...
_____
_____
_____
_____
_____
_____
_____

PRAYER REQUESTS   **ANSWERED PRAYERS**

Today's Affirmation

I mind my own business and wait patiently for the Lord.

Patience

I will replace my worry with prayer and thanksgiving.

> Do not be anxious about anything, but in every situation, by prayer and petition, with thanksgiving, present your requests to God.

PHILIPPIANS 4:6

Daily Devotion

Day 43

Date: ___._____._____

How can I apply this to my life?
_____
_____
_____
_____
_____
_____

What is God saying through this Scripture?
_____
_____
_____
_____
_____
_____

I praise the Lord for...
_____
_____
_____
_____
_____
_____
_____

PRAYER REQUESTS   **ANSWERED PRAYERS**

Today's Affirmation

I don't need to worry about anything, God will help me through everything.

Patience

The battle is not mine but the Lord's.

The Lord will fight for you; you need only to be still."

EXODUS 14:14

Daily Devotion

Day 44

Date: ___._____._____

How can I apply this to my life?
_____
_____
_____
_____
_____
_____

What is God saying through this Scripture?
_____
_____
_____
_____
_____
_____

I praise the Lord for...
_____
_____
_____
_____
_____
_____

PRAYER REQUESTS   **ANSWERED PRAYERS**

Today's Affirmation

I stand firm on God's Word to fight my battles for me and grant me victory.

Patience

He is with me through highs and lows.

Even though I walk through the darkest valley, I will fear no evil, for you are with me; your rod and your staff, they comfort me.

PSALM 23:4

Daily Devotion

Day 45

Date: ___,_____,_____

How can I apply this to my life?
_____
_____
_____
_____
_____
_____

What is God saying through this Scripture?
_____
_____
_____
_____
_____
_____

I praise the Lord for...
_____
_____
_____
_____
_____
_____

PRAYER REQUESTS   **ANSWERED PRAYERS**

Today's Affirmation

I will fear no evil because greater is He that is in me.

Patience

Chosen, holy and dearly loved.

Therefore, as God's chosen people, holy and dearly loved, clothe yourselves with compassion, kindness, humility, gentleness and patience.

COLOSSIANS 3:12

Daily Devotion

Day 46

Date: _____,_____,_____

How can I apply this to my life?
_____
_____
_____
_____
_____
_____

What is God saying through this Scripture?
_____
_____
_____
_____
_____
_____

I praise the Lord for...
_____
_____
_____
_____
_____
_____

PRAYER REQUESTS   **ANSWERED PRAYERS**

Today's Affirmation

I clothe myself with compassion, kindness, humility, gentleness and patience.

Patience

My perseverance will be rewarded.

But as for you, be strong and do not give up, for your work will be rewarded."

2 CHRONICLES 15:7

Daily Devotion

Day 47

Date: ___._____._____

How can I apply this to my life?
_____
_____
_____
_____
_____
_____

What is God saying through this Scripture?
_____
_____
_____
_____
_____
_____

I praise the Lord for...
_____
_____
_____
_____
_____
_____

PRAYER REQUESTS	ANSWERED PRAYERS

Today's Affirmation

I will press on towards God's reward and blessing in my life.

Patience

God is good all the time.

The Lord is good to those whose hope
is in him, to the one who seeks him;
it is good to wait quietly for
the salvation of the Lord.

LAMENTATIONS 3:25-26

Daily Devotion

Day 48

Date: ___,_____,_____

How can I apply this to my life?
_____
_____
_____
_____
_____
_____
_____

What is God saying through this Scripture?
_____
_____
_____
_____
_____
_____
_____

I praise the Lord for...
_____
_____
_____
_____
_____
_____
_____

PRAYER REQUESTS   **ANSWERED PRAYERS**

Today's Affirmation

I will wait upon the Lord because He abounds in goodness and grace.

Patience

God is preparing a table for one

You prepare a table before me in the presence of my enemies. You anoint my head with oil; my cup overflows.

PSALM 23:5

Daily Devotion

Day 49

Date: ____._____,_____

How can I apply this to my life?
_____
_____
_____
_____
_____
_____

What is God saying through this Scripture?
_____
_____
_____
_____
_____
_____

I praise the Lord for...
_____
_____
_____
_____
_____
_____

PRAYER REQUESTS **ANSWERED PRAYERS**

Today's Affirmation

God is about to bless me in the presence of my enemies, my cup will overflow.

Patience

Everything will fall into place at the right time

Jesus replied, "You do not realize now what I am doing, but later you will understand."

JOHN 13:7

Daily Devotion

Day 50

Date: ____,_____,_____

How can I apply this to my life?
_____
_____
_____
_____
_____
_____

What is God saying through this Scripture?
_____
_____
_____
_____
_____
_____

I praise the Lord for...
_____
_____
_____
_____
_____
_____

PRAYER REQUESTS	ANSWERED PRAYERS

Today's Affirmation

I am trusting the process even if I don't understand it right now.

I am prosperous

KINDNESS

Kindness

I overcome evil with good

Do not repay evil with evil or insult with insult. On the contrary, repay evil with blessing, because to this you were called so that you may inherit a blessing.

1 PETER 3:9

Daily Devotion

Day 51

Date: ____._____._____

How can I apply this to my life?
_____
_____
_____
_____
_____
_____

What is God saying through this Scripture?
_____
_____
_____
_____
_____
_____

I praise the Lord for...
_____
_____
_____
_____
_____
_____

PRAYER REQUESTS | ANSWERED PRAYERS

Today's Affirmation

I will repay evil with a blessing and the Lord will bless me for my act of kindness.

Kindness

I will show others my God-given heart.

Do to others as you would have them do to you.

LUKE 6:31

Daily Devotion

Day 52

Date: ____,_____,____

How can I apply this to my life?
_____
_____
_____
_____
_____
_____

What is God saying through this Scripture?
_____
_____
_____
_____
_____
_____

I praise the Lord for...
_____
_____
_____
_____
_____
_____

PRAYER REQUESTS   **ANSWERED PRAYERS**

Today's Affirmation

I will treat others the way I want to be treated; with love, kindness and respect.

Kindness

I will choose my words wisely, they have the power to hurt or heal.

> *Anxiety weighs down the heart, but a kind word cheers it up.*
>
> PROVERBS 12:25

Daily Devotion

Day 53

Date: ___._____._____

How can I apply this to my life?
_____
_____
_____
_____
_____
_____

What is God saying through this Scripture?
_____
_____
_____
_____
_____
_____

I praise the Lord for...
_____
_____
_____
_____
_____
_____

PRAYER REQUESTS | **ANSWERED PRAYERS**

Today's Affirmation

I choose to think and speak kind words towards myself and others.

Kindness

I will do what the Lord requires of me

He has shown you, O mortal, what is good.
And what does the Lord require of you?
To act justly and to love mercy and to walk
humbly with your God.

MICAH 6:8

Daily Devotion

Day 54

Date: ___._____._____

How can I apply this to my life?
_____
_____
_____
_____
_____
_____
_____

What is God saying through this Scripture?
_____
_____
_____
_____
_____
_____
_____

I praise the Lord for...
_____
_____
_____
_____
_____
_____
_____

PRAYER REQUESTS   **ANSWERED PRAYERS**

Today's Affirmation

My God is a God of justice and mercy, I will walk humbly with Him.

Kindness

God shows favour to the humble.

Humble yourselves, therefore,
under God's mighty hand,
that he may lift you up in due time.

1 PETER 5:6

Daily Devotion

Day 55

Date: ____._____._____

How can I apply this to my life?
_____
_____
_____
_____
_____
_____

What is God saying through this Scripture?
_____
_____
_____
_____
_____
_____

I praise the Lord for...
_____
_____
_____
_____
_____
_____

PRAYER REQUESTS	ANSWERED PRAYERS

Today's Affirmation

I humble myself before God as He will exult me in due season.

Kindness

My kind words have the ability to heal.

> Gracious words are a honeycomb, sweet to the soul and healing to the bones.
>
> PROVERBS 16:24

Daily Devotion

Day 56

Date: ___._____._____

How can I apply this to my life?
_____
_____
_____
_____
_____

What is God saying through this Scripture?
_____
_____
_____
_____
_____

I praise the Lord for...
_____
_____
_____
_____
_____

PRAYER REQUESTS   **ANSWERED PRAYERS**

Today's Affirmation

When I am kind, I bring healing to my own soul and to those around me.

Kindness

I send out love and kindness, and that's what I receive back.

Whoever pursues righteousness and love finds life, prosperity and honor.

PROVERBS 21:21

Daily Devotion

Day 57

Date: ___,_____,_____

How can I apply this to my life?
_____
_____
_____
_____
_____
_____

What is God saying through this Scripture?
_____
_____
_____
_____
_____
_____

I praise the Lord for...
_____
_____
_____
_____
_____
_____

PRAYER REQUESTS   **ANSWERED PRAYERS**

Today's Affirmation

I know I will get what I put out there, so I choose to always be kind.

Kindness

Being kind to others is rewarding.

Those who are kind benefit themselves, but the cruel bring ruin on themselves.

PROVERBS 11:17

Daily Devotion

Day 58

Date: ____,_____,_____

How can I apply this to my life?
_____
_____
_____
_____
_____
_____

What is God saying through this Scripture?
_____
_____
_____
_____
_____
_____

I praise the Lord for...
_____
_____
_____
_____
_____
_____

PRAYER REQUESTS   **ANSWERED PRAYERS**

Today's Affirmation

My kindness and gratitude to others and life will make my heart happy.

Kindness

I will do good and hate what is evil.

But love your enemies, do good to them, and lend to them without expecting to get anything back. Then your reward will be great, and you will be children of the Most High, because he is kind to the ungrateful and wicked.

LUKE 6:35

Daily Devotion

Day 59

Date: ____,_____,_____

How can I apply this to my life?
_____
_____
_____
_____
_____
_____

What is God saying through this Scripture?
_____
_____
_____
_____
_____
_____

I praise the Lord for...
_____
_____
_____
_____
_____
_____

PRAYER REQUESTS   **ANSWERED PRAYERS**

Today's Affirmation

The Lord will bless me abundantly as I continue to do good.

Kindness

Being kind to others uplifts my soul and makes one happy.

On the contrary: "If your enemy is hungry, feed him; if he is thirsty, give him something to drink. In doing this, you will heap burning coals on his head." Do not be overcome by evil, but overcome evil with good.

ROMANS 12:20-21

Daily Devotion

Day 60

Date: ____._____._____

How can I apply this to my life?
_____
_____
_____
_____
_____
_____

What is God saying through this Scripture?
_____
_____
_____
_____
_____
_____

I praise the Lord for...
_____
_____
_____
_____
_____
_____

PRAYER REQUESTS   **ANSWERED PRAYERS**

Today's Affirmation

I will show love and kindness to others just as God is kind and loving towards me.

I am loved

PEACE

Peace

I will overcome everything just as Christ has overcome the world.

I have told you these things, so that in me you may have peace. In this world you will have trouble. But take heart! I have overcome the world.

JOHN 16:33

Daily Devotion

Day 61

Date: ____._____._____

How can I apply this to my life?
_____
_____
_____
_____
_____

What is God saying through this Scripture?
_____
_____
_____
_____
_____

I praise the Lord for...
_____
_____
_____
_____
_____

PRAYER REQUESTS   **ANSWERED PRAYERS**

Today's Affirmation

In Christ I have peace and in Him I find rest for my soul even in the midst of my storm.

Peace

*His peace transcends
all understanding.*

And the peace of God, which transcends all understanding, will guard your hearts and your minds in Christ Jesus.

PHILIPPIANS 4:7

Daily Devotion

Day 62

Date: ___,_____,_____

How can I apply this to my life?
_____
_____
_____
_____
_____
_____

What is God saying through this Scripture?
_____
_____
_____
_____
_____
_____

I praise the Lord for...
_____
_____
_____
_____
_____
_____

PRAYER REQUESTS   **ANSWERED PRAYERS**

Today's Affirmation

God's peace will guard my heart and mind in Christ Jesus.

Peace

I will keep my tongue from evil and seek peace instead.

> Whoever would love life and see good days must keep their tongue from evil and their lips from deceitful speech. They must turn from evil and do good; they must seek peace and pursue it.

1 PETER 3:10-11

Daily Devotion

Day 63

Date: ___,_____,_____

How can I apply this to my life?
_____
_____
_____
_____
_____
_____

What is God saying through this Scripture?
_____
_____
_____
_____
_____
_____

I praise the Lord for...
_____
_____
_____
_____
_____
_____

PRAYER REQUESTS   **ANSWERED PRAYERS**

Today's Affirmation

I will do good and pursue peace that I may see good days in my life.

Peace

I will not seek revenge because it is His to avenge.

If it is possible, as far as it depends on you, live at peace with everyone. Do not take revenge, my dear friends, but leave room for God's wrath, for it is written: "It is mine to avenge; I will repay," says the Lord.

ROMANS 12:18-19

Daily Devotion

Day 64

Date: ____,_____,_____

How can I apply this to my life?
_____
_____
_____
_____
_____
_____
_____

What is God saying through this Scripture?
_____
_____
_____
_____
_____
_____
_____

I praise the Lord for...
_____
_____
_____
_____
_____
_____
_____

PRAYER REQUESTS   **ANSWERED PRAYERS**

Today's Affirmation

God is a God of justice, He will repay.

Peace

In Him I find rest for my soul.

> Come to me, all you who are weary and
> burdened, and I will give you rest.
> Take my yoke upon you and learn from me,
> for I am gentle and humble in heart,
> and you will find rest for your souls.
> For my yoke is easy and my burden is light.
>
> MATTHEW 11:28-30

Daily Devotion

Day 65

Date: ___,_____,_____

How can I apply this to my life?
_____
_____
_____
_____
_____
_____

What is God saying through this Scripture?
_____
_____
_____
_____
_____
_____

I praise the Lord for...
_____
_____
_____
_____
_____
_____

PRAYER REQUESTS　　　　**ANSWERED PRAYERS**

Today's Affirmation

The Lord will give me rest as I surrender all my troubles to Him.

Peace

He strengthens me,
He gives me peace.

The Lord gives strength to his people; the Lord blesses his people with peace.

PSALM 29:11

Daily Devotion

Day 66

Date: ___,_____,_____

How can I apply this to my life?
_____
_____
_____
_____
_____
_____

What is God saying through this Scripture?
_____
_____
_____
_____
_____
_____

I praise the Lord for...
_____
_____
_____
_____
_____
_____

PRAYER REQUESTS   **ANSWERED PRAYERS**

Today's Affirmation

The Lord gives me strength and blesses me with peace everywhere I go.

Peace

I will let the peace of Christ rule my heart

Let the peace of Christ rule in your hearts, since as members of one body you were called to peace. And be thankful.

COLOSSIANS 3:15

Daily Devotion

Day 67

Date: ___._____._____

How can I apply this to my life?
_____
_____
_____
_____
_____
_____

What is God saying through this Scripture?
_____
_____
_____
_____
_____
_____

I praise the Lord for...
_____
_____
_____
_____
_____
_____

PRAYER REQUESTS   **ANSWERED PRAYERS**

Today's Affirmation

I am thankful for what I have and at peace with where I am right now.

Peace

*As a child of God
I choose to be a peacemaker.*

Blessed are the peacemakers, for they will be called children of God. Blessed are those who are persecuted because of righteousness, for theirs is the kingdom of heaven.

MATTHEW 5:9-10

Daily Devotion

Day 68

Date: ___,_____,_____

How can I apply this to my life?
_____
_____
_____
_____
_____
_____

What is God saying through this Scripture?
_____
_____
_____
_____
_____
_____

I praise the Lord for...
_____
_____
_____
_____
_____
_____

PRAYER REQUESTS   **ANSWERED PRAYERS**

Today's Affirmation

I am a child of God and the kingdom of heaven is mine through Jesus Christ.

Peace

The Lord cares about me.

Cast all your anxiety on him because he cares for you.

1 PETER 5:7

Daily Devotion — Day 69

Date: ___,_____,_____

How can I apply this to my life?
_____
_____
_____
_____
_____

What is God saying through this Scripture?
_____
_____
_____
_____
_____

I praise the Lord for...
_____
_____
_____
_____
_____

PRAYER REQUESTS   **ANSWERED PRAYERS**

Today's Affirmation

I cast all my anxiety on Him because He loves me and cares for me.

Peace

The peace Christ gives one cannot be found in the world.

Peace I leave with you; my peace I give you.
I do not give to you as the world gives.
Do not let your hearts be troubled and do
not be afraid.

JOHN 14:27

Daily Devotion

Day 70

Date: ___._____._____

How can I apply this to my life?
_____
_____
_____
_____
_____
_____
_____

What is God saying through this Scripture?
_____
_____
_____
_____
_____
_____
_____

I praise the Lord for...
_____
_____
_____
_____
_____
_____
_____

PRAYER REQUESTS

ANSWERED PRAYERS

Today's Affirmation

The Prince of Peace is with me, I will not be afraid of let my heart be troubled.

I am healthy

JOY

Joy

His joy is in me.

If you keep my commands, you will remain in my love, just as I have kept my Father's commands and remain in his love. I have told you this so that my joy may be in you and that your joy may be complete.

JOHN 15:10-11

Daily Devotion

Day 71

Date: ____._____,_____

How can I apply this to my life?
_____
_____
_____
_____
_____
_____

What is God saying through this Scripture?
_____
_____
_____
_____
_____
_____

I praise the Lord for...
_____
_____
_____
_____
_____
_____

PRAYER REQUESTS   **ANSWERED PRAYERS**

Today's Affirmation

As I keep His commands and remain in His love, His joy in me will be complete.

Joy

I experience true joy in the presence of the Lord.

You make known to me the path of life; you will fill me with joy in your presence, with eternal pleasures at your right hand.

PSALM 16:11

Daily Devotion

Day 72

Date: ____,_____,_____

How can I apply this to my life?
_____
_____
_____
_____
_____
_____

What is God saying through this Scripture?
_____
_____
_____
_____
_____
_____

I praise the Lord for...
_____
_____
_____
_____
_____
_____

PRAYER REQUESTS   **ANSWERED PRAYERS**

Today's Affirmation

When I commune with God, I am filled by the eternal joy of His sweet presence.

Joy

He is doing a good thing in one.

Consider it pure joy, my brothers and sisters, whenever you face trials of many kinds, because you know that the testing of your faith produces perseverance. Let perseverance finish its work so that you may be mature and complete, not lacking anything.

JAMES 1:2-4

Daily Devotion

Day 73

Date: ___,_____,_____

How can I apply this to my life?
_____
_____
_____
_____
_____
_____

What is God saying through this Scripture?
_____
_____
_____
_____
_____
_____

I praise the Lord for...
_____
_____
_____
_____
_____
_____

PRAYER REQUESTS **ANSWERED PRAYERS**

Today's Affirmation

God will use my trials to make me stronger in faith, lacking in nothing.

Joy

My heart is filled with joy when my prayers are answered

May we shout for joy over your victory
and lift up our banners in the name
of our God. May the Lord grant
all your requests.

PSALM 20:4-5

Daily Devotion

Day 74

Date: ___,_____,_____

How can I apply this to my life?
_____
_____
_____
_____
_____
_____
_____

What is God saying through this Scripture?
_____
_____
_____
_____
_____
_____
_____

I praise the Lord for...
_____
_____
_____
_____
_____
_____
_____

PRAYER REQUESTS   **ANSWERED PRAYERS**

Today's Affirmation

I am victorious, I shout for joy and praise His Holy name.

Joy

God is about to enlarge me for His blessing.

You have enlarged the nation and increased their joy; they rejoice before you as people rejoice at the harvest, as warriors rejoice when dividing the plunder.

ISAIAH 9:3

Daily Devotion

Day 75

Date: ____,_____,_____

How can I apply this to my life?
_____
_____
_____
_____
_____
_____

What is God saying through this Scripture?
_____
_____
_____
_____
_____
_____

I praise the Lord for...
_____
_____
_____
_____
_____
_____

PRAYER REQUESTS   **ANSWERED PRAYERS**

Today's Affirmation

God is about to bless me abundantly and increase my joy. In Him I have put my trust.

Joy

In due time my grief will be replaced with everlasting joy.

So with you: Now is your time of grief, but I will see you again and you will rejoice, and no one will take away your joy.

JOHN 16:22

Daily Devotion

Day 76

Date: ___._____._____

How can I apply this to my life?
_____
_____
_____
_____
_____

What is God saying through this Scripture?
_____
_____
_____
_____
_____

I praise the Lord for...
_____
_____
_____
_____
_____

PRAYER REQUESTS   **ANSWERED PRAYERS**

Today's Affirmation

I will not give up because what God has for me is worth the wait.

Joy

No matter how dark the night, joy will always come in the morning.

> For his anger lasts only a moment, but his favor lasts a lifetime; weeping may stay for the night, but rejoicing comes in the morning.
>
> PSALM 30:5

Daily Devotion

Day 77

Date: ____._____._____

How can I apply this to my life?
_____
_____
_____
_____
_____
_____

What is God saying through this Scripture?
_____
_____
_____
_____
_____
_____

I praise the Lord for...
_____
_____
_____
_____
_____
_____

PRAYER REQUESTS	ANSWERED PRAYERS

Today's Affirmation

The struggle never lasts, His joy awaits me every new day.

Joy

The Lord will crown one with everlasting joy.

and those the Lord has rescued will return. They will enter Zion with singing; everlasting joy will crown their heads. Gladness and joy will overtake them, and sorrow and sighing will flee away.

ISAIAH 35:10

Daily Devotion

Day 78

Date: ___,_____,_____

How can I apply this to my life?
_____
_____
_____
_____
_____
_____

What is God saying through this Scripture?
_____
_____
_____
_____
_____
_____

I praise the Lord for...
_____
_____
_____
_____
_____
_____

PRAYER REQUESTS	ANSWERED PRAYERS

Today's Affirmation

My pain is only temporary because everlasting joy and gladness will overtake me.

Joy

My joy can only be found in the Lord.

Though you have not seen him, you love him; and even though you do not see him now, you believe in him and are filled with an inexpressible and glorious joy, for you are receiving the end result of your faith, the salvation of your souls.

1 PETER 1:8-9

Daily Devotion

Day 79

Date: ___._____._____

How can I apply this to my life?
_____
_____
_____
_____
_____
_____

What is God saying through this Scripture?
_____
_____
_____
_____
_____
_____

I praise the Lord for...
_____
_____
_____
_____
_____
_____

PRAYER REQUESTS   **ANSWERED PRAYERS**

Today's Affirmation

The Lord is always with me and He fills my soul with an inexpressible and glorious joy.

Joy

Pure joy and bliss is coming my way.

I consider that our present sufferings are not worth comparing with the glory that will be revealed in us.

ROMANS 8:18

Daily Devotion

Day 80

Date: ___,_____,_____

How can I apply this to my life?
_____
_____
_____
_____
_____
_____

What is God saying through this Scripture?
_____
_____
_____
_____
_____
_____

I praise the Lord for...
_____
_____
_____
_____
_____
_____

PRAYER REQUESTS   **ANSWERED PRAYERS**

Today's Affirmation

Where I am today is leading me to where I want to be.

I am happy

Courage

God will never fail me or abandon me.

No one will be able to stand against you all the days of your life. As I was with Moses, so I will be with you; I will never leave you nor forsake you.

JOSHUA 1:5

Daily Devotion

Day 81

Date: ___,_____,_____

How can I apply this to my life?
_____
_____
_____
_____
_____
_____

What is God saying through this Scripture?
_____
_____
_____
_____
_____
_____

I praise the Lord for...
_____
_____
_____
_____
_____
_____

PRAYER REQUESTS	ANSWERED PRAYERS

Today's Affirmation

God will never leave me nor forsake me, I am never alone.

Courage

The Lord provides the refuge and shelter my soul seeks.

He will cover you with his feathers, and under his wings you will find refuge; his faithfulness will be your shield and rampart.

PSALM 91:4

Daily Devotion

Day 82

Date: ___,_____,_____

How can I apply this to my life?
_____
_____
_____
_____
_____
_____

What is God saying through this Scripture?
_____
_____
_____
_____
_____
_____

I praise the Lord for...
_____
_____
_____
_____
_____
_____

PRAYER REQUESTS   **ANSWERED PRAYERS**

Today's Affirmation

I'm never alone, I can always hide under His wings.

Courage

My heart trusts in Him.

> The Lord is my strength and my shield; my heart trusts in him, and he helps me. My heart leaps for joy, and with my song I praise him.

PSALM 28:7

Daily Devotion

Day 83

Date: ___._____._____

How can I apply this to my life?
_____
_____
_____
_____
_____
_____

What is God saying through this Scripture?
_____
_____
_____
_____
_____
_____

I praise the Lord for...
_____
_____
_____
_____
_____
_____

PRAYER REQUESTS

ANSWERED PRAYERS

Today's Affirmation

The Lord is my strength and shield, I trust in Him.

Courage

Instead of fear, God gives one the Spirit of power.

For the Spirit God gave us does not make us timid, but gives us power, love and self-discipline.

2 TIMOTHY 1:7

Daily Devotion

Day 84

Date: ___._____,_____

How can I apply this to my life?
_____
_____
_____
_____
_____
_____

What is God saying through this Scripture?
_____
_____
_____
_____
_____
_____

I praise the Lord for...
_____
_____
_____
_____
_____
_____

PRAYER REQUESTS   **ANSWERED PRAYERS**

Today's Affirmation

The Spirit of God makes me strong and courageous

Courage

He is with one till the end of times.

And teaching them to obey everything I have commanded you.
And surely I am with you always, to the very end of the age.

MATTHEW 28:20

Daily Devotion

Day 85

Date: ___,_____,_____

How can I apply this to my life?
_____
_____
_____
_____
_____
_____

What is God saying through this Scripture?
_____
_____
_____
_____
_____
_____

I praise the Lord for...
_____
_____
_____
_____
_____
_____

PRAYER REQUESTS　　　　**ANSWERED PRAYERS**

Today's Affirmation

I fear nothing because the Lord is with me always.

Courage

With Him all things are possible.

Jesus looked at them and said, "With man this is impossible, but with God all things are possible.

MATTHEW 19:26

Daily Devotion Day 86

Date: ___._____,_____

How can I apply this to my life?
_____
_____
_____
_____
_____
_____

What is God saying through this Scripture?
_____
_____
_____
_____
_____
_____

I praise the Lord for...
_____
_____
_____
_____
_____
_____

PRAYER REQUESTS   **ANSWERED PRAYERS**

Today's Affirmation

I am bold and courageous because with God all things are made possible.

Courage

My safety is important to God.

For he will command his angels
concerning you to guard you
in all your ways;

PSALM 91:11

Daily Devotion

Day 87

Date: ___._____,_____

How can I apply this to my life?
_____
_____
_____
_____
_____
_____

What is God saying through this Scripture?
_____
_____
_____
_____
_____
_____

I praise the Lord for...
_____
_____
_____
_____
_____
_____

PRAYER REQUESTS   **ANSWERED PRAYERS**

Today's Affirmation

I have nothing to fear, God commands the angels to guard me.

Courage

The Lord is always with me.

So do not fear, for I am with you; do not be dismayed, for I am your God. I will strengthen you and help you; I will uphold you with my righteous right hand.

ISAIAH 41:10

Daily Devotion

Day 88

Date: ___,_____,_____

How can I apply this to my life?
_____
_____
_____
_____
_____
_____

What is God saying through this Scripture?
_____
_____
_____
_____
_____
_____

I praise the Lord for...
_____
_____
_____
_____
_____
_____

PRAYER REQUESTS

ANSWERED PRAYERS

Today's Affirmation

I will not fear because God upholds me with His righteous right hand.

Courage

I will be courageous and wait for the Lord

*Wait for the Lord;
be strong and take heart
and wait for the Lord.*

PSALM 27:14

Daily Devotion

Day 89

Date: ___,_____,_____

How can I apply this to my life?
_____
_____
_____
_____
_____
_____

What is God saying through this Scripture?
_____
_____
_____
_____
_____
_____

I praise the Lord for...
_____
_____
_____
_____
_____
_____

PRAYER REQUESTS   **ANSWERED PRAYERS**

Today's Affirmation

I will not let fear control me, I will stand firm in faith and wait for the Lord.

Courage

I am strong and courageous.

Be strong and courageous. Do not be afraid or terrified because of them, for the LORD your God goes with you; he will never leave you nor forsake you.

DEUTERONOMY 31:6

Daily Devotion

Day 90

Date: ___._____,_____

How can I apply this to my life?

_____
_____
_____
_____
_____
_____
_____

What is God saying through this Scripture?

_____
_____
_____
_____
_____
_____
_____

I praise the Lord for...

_____
_____
_____
_____
_____
_____
_____

PRAYER REQUESTS   **ANSWERED PRAYERS**

Today's Affirmation

The Lord, my God, goes with me wherever I go.

I am courageous

FORGIVENESS

Forgiveness

My God is gracious and forgiving.

Come now, let us settle the matter," says the Lord. "Though your sins are like scarlet, they shall be as white as snow; though they are red as crimson, they shall be like wool.

ISAIAH 1:18

Daily Devotion

Day 91

Date: ____,_____,____

How can I apply this to my life?
_____
_____
_____
_____
_____
_____

What is God saying through this Scripture?
_____
_____
_____
_____
_____
_____

I praise the Lord for...
_____
_____
_____
_____
_____
_____

PRAYER REQUESTS   **ANSWERED PRAYERS**

Today's Affirmation

Repentance leads me to God's forgiveness, I have been forgiven.

Forgiveness

I aim to live a life pleasing to God.

Get rid of all bitterness, rage and anger, brawling and slander, along with every form of malice. Be kind and compassionate to one another, forgiving each other, just as in Christ God forgave you.

EPHESIANS 4:31-32

Daily Devotion

Day 92

Date: ___._____._____

How can I apply this to my life?
_____
_____
_____
_____
_____
_____

What is God saying through this Scripture?
_____
_____
_____
_____
_____
_____

I praise the Lord for...
_____
_____
_____
_____
_____
_____

PRAYER REQUESTS   **ANSWERED PRAYERS**

Today's Affirmation

Today I choose to let go of all bitterness. I forgive those who have hurt me.

Forgiveness

I am developing a forgiving heart like His.

> Do not judge, and you
> will not be judged. Do not condemn,
> and you will not be condemned.
> Forgive, and you will be forgiven.
>
> LUKE 6:37

Daily Devotion

Day 93

Date: ____,_____,_____

How can I apply this to my life?
_____
_____
_____
_____
_____

What is God saying through this Scripture?
_____
_____
_____
_____
_____
_____

I praise the Lord for...
_____
_____
_____
_____
_____
_____

PRAYER REQUESTS   **ANSWERED PRAYERS**

Today's Affirmation

I will not judge others so I am not judged. I forgive as I have been forgiven.

Forgiveness

I humble myself and admit my own mistakes.

If we confess our sins, he is faithful and just and will forgive us our sins and purify us from all unrighteousness.

1 JOHN 1:9

Daily Devotion

Day 94

Date: ___,_____,____

How can I apply this to my life?
_____
_____
_____
_____
_____
_____

What is God saying through this Scripture?
_____
_____
_____
_____
_____
_____

I praise the Lord for...
_____
_____
_____
_____
_____
_____

PRAYER REQUESTS   **ANSWERED PRAYERS**

Today's Affirmation

The Lord is faithful and just to forgive me when I repent.

Forgiveness

I am not perfect, but I'm blessed to be forgiven.

Blessed are those whose transgressions are forgiven, whose sins are covered. Blessed is the one whose sin the Lord will never count against them.

ROMANS 4:7-8

Daily Devotion

Day 95

Date: ___._____,_____

How can I apply this to my life?
_____
_____
_____
_____
_____

What is God saying through this Scripture?
_____
_____
_____
_____
_____

I praise the Lord for...
_____
_____
_____
_____
_____

PRAYER REQUESTS

ANSWERED PRAYERS

Today's Affirmation

God doesn't expect me to be perfect, He wants me to be better.

Forgiveness

The Lord remembers my sins no more.

"I, even I, am he who blots out your transgressions, for my own sake, and remembers your sins no more.

ISAIAH 43:25

Daily Devotion

Day 96

Date: ___._____._____

How can I apply this to my life?
_____
_____
_____
_____
_____
_____

What is God saying through this Scripture?
_____
_____
_____
_____
_____
_____

I praise the Lord for...
_____
_____
_____
_____
_____
_____

PRAYER REQUESTS   **ANSWERED PRAYERS**

Today's Affirmation

I am free from condemnation, the Lord has wiped out my sins.

Forgiveness

*I will not hide behind my pride,
I know I need forgiveness.*

> Whoever conceals their sins does not prosper, but the one who confesses and renounces them finds mercy.
>
> PROVERBS 28:13

Daily Devotion

Day 97

Date: ___, _____, _____

How can I apply this to my life?
_____
_____
_____
_____
_____
_____

What is God saying through this Scripture?
_____
_____
_____
_____
_____
_____

I praise the Lord for...
_____
_____
_____
_____
_____
_____

PRAYER REQUESTS   **ANSWERED PRAYERS**

Today's Affirmation

I find mercy and forgiveness every time I confess my sins.

Forgiveness

Forgiveness will set me free.

And when you stand praying, if you hold anything against anyone, forgive them, so that your Father in heaven may forgive you your sins.

MARK 11:25

Daily Devotion

Day 98

Date: ____._____._____

How can I apply this to my life?
_____
_____
_____
_____
_____

What is God saying through this Scripture?
_____
_____
_____
_____
_____

I praise the Lord for...
_____
_____
_____
_____
_____

PRAYER REQUESTS

ANSWERED PRAYERS

Today's Affirmation

Forgiveness sets me free from the pain, I choose to be free.

Forgiveness

I have been redeemed from darkness to light.

For he has rescued us from the dominion of darkness and brought us into the kingdom of the Son he loves, in whom we have redemption, the forgiveness of sins.

COLOSSIANS 1:13-14

Daily Devotion

Day 99

Date: ____,_____,_____

How can I apply this to my life?
_____
_____
_____
_____
_____
_____

What is God saying through this Scripture?
_____
_____
_____
_____
_____
_____

I praise the Lord for...
_____
_____
_____
_____
_____
_____

PRAYER REQUESTS	ANSWERED PRAYERS

Today's Affirmation

He who loved me rescued me from darkness to light, I am redeemed.

Forgiveness

Who is a God like you?

> Who is a God like you, who pardons sin and forgives the transgression of the remnant of his inheritance? You do not stay angry forever but delight to show mercy. You will again have compassion on us; you will tread our sins underfoot and hurl all our iniquities into the depths of the sea.
>
> **MICAH 7:18-19**

Daily Devotion

Day 100

Date: ___,_____,_____

How can I apply this to my life?
_____
_____
_____
_____
_____
_____

What is God saying through this Scripture?
_____
_____
_____
_____
_____
_____

I praise the Lord for...
_____
_____
_____
_____
_____
_____

PRAYER REQUESTS

ANSWERED PRAYERS

Today's Affirmation

God is full of compassion and mercy, He pardons my sins and forgives my transgressions.

I am protected

Sometimes God takes away something you never expected losing, but He will replace it with something you never imagined having.

**But as Scripture says:
"No eye has seen,
no ear has heard,
and no mind has imagined
the things that God has prepared
for those who love him."**
1 Corinthians 2:9

My Notes

Date: ___._____._____

My Notes

Date: ___,_____,_____

My Notes

Date: ____,_____,_____

My Notes

Date: ____,_____,_____

My Notes

Date: ___,_____,_____

My Notes

Date: _____._____,_____

My Notes

Date: ___,_____,_____

My Notes

Date: ___,_____,_____

My Notes

Date: ___,_____,_____

My Notes

Date: ___,_____,_____

I am joyful

About the Author

Noor Niami is an author, spiritual mentor and speaker but above all she is a woman of God and a believer. Christ alone defines the woman she is and her identity is built purely on Him. Her passion to help others has become her purpose in life and she is determined to empower those who have been hurt and heal the broken-hearted by sharing her personal journey and experiences. Coming from a place of brokenness herself she knows what it feels like to be in that dark place desperately waiting to see the light at the end of the tunnel. It wasn't until she refused to wait any longer and decided to become the light she needed instead. And from there on her mission to empower people around the world began. She is determined to be a living testimony to God's unfailing love, grace, and mercy. And she wants to assure you that the pain you've been feeling now can't compare to the joy that is coming.

For more information visit:
www.noorniami.com